Tasks Galore

For The Real World

- ❖ Valuable for preparing your exceptional student for the "Real World"
- ❖ Full-color pictorial series of visually structured tasks for teaching domestic, vocational and other independent living skills to individuals with autism
- ❖ Applicable to home, school, and community, training sites

Laurie Eckenrode, Pat Fennell, and Kathy Hearsey

Acknowledgements

Throughout our careers, staff of Division TEACCH (**T**reatment and **E**ducation of **A**utistic and related **C**ommunication handicapped **Ch**ildren) have taught, encouraged, and inspired us. We will forever admire the services they provide. Partial proceeds from the sale of this book will help support the continuing efforts of Division TEACCH. Many people have helped us bring our vision of *Tasks Galore for the Real World* into focus. Among these we thank Kaitlin, Kat, and David Moncol for their never-ending enthusiasm, Tracy Serviss for opening her classroom doors, Tim and Terry Davis of Landmark Printing for continued support of projects that enhance the lives of people with autism, Doug Fennell for his photographic expertise, Michelle Jordy for her technical assistance, and John Barton for his editorial guidance. We give special thanks to our friends with autism spectrum disorder for allowing us to share in their journey.

About the Authors

Laurie Eckenrode, is a veteran lead teacher in a self-contained program for young children with autism and serves as a trainer for Division TEACCH.

Pat Fennell, formerly a teacher, recently retired from Division TEACCH, where she was a psycho-educational therapist and trainer.

Kathy Hearsey, also formerly a teacher, works for Division TEACCH as a psycho-educational therapist and trainer. She also served as the director of supported employment for Division TEACCH.

Laurie, Pat, and Kathy have all provided training across the United States, as well as abroad. They have won many awards for their achievements in the field of special education. Together, Laurie, Pat, and Kathy have over 60 years of experience working with exceptional children and adults.

Table of Contents

INTRODUCTION

The authors proudly present *Tasks Galore for the Real World*, the second in a series of task books for people with autism spectrum disorders and other visual learners. The goal of our books is to provide parents, teachers, and therapists with ideas for creating tasks for students who benefit from multi-modal presentations, which incorporate visual, tactile, and motor movement components. This type of task captures the interest of most students and enables them to sustain their attention in learning. Often, many students who have not been too successful understanding concepts taught in traditional ways can excel in the tasks presented in the *Tasks Galore* series. The tasks depicted in *Tasks Galore for the Real World* emphasize a functional approach, focusing on concepts needed to manage independently in life and on skills that can open vocational possibilities.

WHY A FUNCTIONAL APPROACH IS IMPORTANT

Students with autism often have excellent ability to memorize. This strength deceives caregivers into believing that concepts underlying the memorized facts and procedures are present. Some students, for example, may easily learn to subtract on a math worksheet, but not understand they must subtract to make sure they have enough money for a purchase. A functional approach involves constantly asking whether students have learned the concepts that underlie their memorized knowledge. Such an approach establishes visual structure within tasks to enable students to perform certain jobs, even though they have not yet developed the underlying conceptual understanding. Students developing typically recognize situations in which they need to use their reading, writing, math, reasoning, fine-motor, and other learned skills. Students, dealing with the challenges of autism, however, usually need to be taught specifically how to generalize their knowledge. Of necessity, therefore, a functional approach requires a student with autism to take learning experiences beyond a desk. The larger world becomes the classroom as the student applies learned tasks to naturally occurring environments in which those skills have a direct purpose.

HOW STRUCTURED TEACHING STRATEGIES HELP

Learning and feeling at ease in a larger world can be a challenge for students with autism. One of the reasons for their confusion and discomfort is that they usually struggle with using and understanding language. Typically, they lack an intuitive social sense, so they do not know instinctively what is expected. Additionally, they see all stimuli in a task or situation as equally important, sometimes finding even the insignificant, such as the flooring pattern, more interesting and understandable than the job to be done. Our experiences, working with Division TEACCH, a statewide program for people with autism spectrum disorders and their families, have taught us the usefulness of structured teaching strategies to minimize discomfort and confusion. Parents, teachers, therapists, psychologists, and others associated with the TEACCH program over the past 40+ years of its existence have developed structured teaching strategies based on watching thousands of children diagnosed with autism grow up and become adults. These long-term observations have enabled us to see which strategies work, and, as importantly, which ones do not. Determining which strategies will allow students to become as successful as possible in life after school evolves continually as we watch the children develop.

Based on these long-term observations, we strongly believe most students reach their greatest level of independent functioning when caregivers implement the following structural aspects:
>   physical structure,
>   daily schedule, and
>   work system or "to do" list.

With structure, students are better able to apply their learning, cope with the real world environment, and perform jobs outside of the classroom. We encourage you to teach your students how to use these aspects of structure independently before venturing into bewildering settings.

PHYSICAL STRUCTURE

Physical structure refers to the way the environmental setting can be adapted so that the students can more easily focus on significant details. Even rearranging furniture and organizing materials can add meaning to the context. Setting up specific areas at home or school where activities take place and defining these areas with clear visual and physical boundaries help students attach the appropriate expectations: here I work; here I relax; here I eat; here I exercise; etc. Physical boundaries in a setting, such as a partition to block out a computer screen, enable a student to screen out distracting stimuli.

THE DAILY SCHEDULE

By the time that parents and teachers are planning more functional teaching for their students in a variety of settings, the students already will have learned how to use daily schedules independently and successfully. A schedule outlines for the student what activities will occur and in what sequence. It tells the student where to go and what is next. If a student can learn the essential routine of following the schedule, he or she can become less dependent on continual directions. From students who have learned to make their own daily schedules to students who still need a concrete object (e.g., spoon means lunch) given to them, a well-learned routine of following a daily schedule opens doors to more independence, with greater flexibility in new surroundings and with new authority figures. Although a daily schedule includes activities that the student chooses, following it routinely assures that the student is receptive to the essential activities of daily life. Everyone has to follow some sort of schedule to be successful in life; that is just one of the "ways of the world". Often, teachers will feel that, because their students have learned the classroom schedule, they no longer need an individualized schedule. With our students, however, we have seen that a daily schedule, routinely used and adjusted as the student develops, is a vital stepping stone to independence beyond the classroom walls.

THE WORK SYSTEM OR "TO DO" LIST

Just as the students first learned to use a daily schedule in a classroom or home setting before applying their skills in real life settings, they must be taught to use their work system independently before applying it broadly. A work system provides a systematic way to approach the work that needs to be done. A work system answers, "Ok, now I am here at the grocery store, what am I supposed to do?" Without a to do list in place and without a well-practiced, independent routine of using it, the situation will feel overwhelming to persons with autism. It is unlikely they will feel competent if they do not have answered in visual ways the following four questions.

1. What work?
2. How much work?
3. How do I know I am making progress and when I am finished?
4. What happens next?

INVESTIGATING THE NEW SETTING

When teaching in a community location, we give much thought to what naturally occurring features can be used to provide physical structure or to answer some work system questions. Prior to working with students in new surroundings, we strongly recommend that caregivers visit and reconnoiter the setting. Then using knowledge about how people with autism think and process information, teachers and parents can hypothesize what will be distracting, confusing, or overwhelming. In addition, using knowledge about structured teaching strategies helps determine how to set up the initial physical structure, schedule, work system, and task in the community location.

COMMUNICATING FUNCTIONALLY

A functional approach means we evaluate our students' ability to communicate important needs. Even with copious vocabularies, some students we know cannot properly select which words to use, nor when to use them. We teach students to communicate these functional needs first in the classroom in a manner that is meaningful. We teach students to use objects, pictures, photographs, written and spoken words, or some combination to communicate pragmatically. After successfully communicating in the classroom, the students can be expected to generalize this skill to the wider world. Our long-term observations have taught us some of the communication needs important in real world situations:

help,
clarification,
missing or more materials,
a bathroom break,
escape from a stressful situation,
work to be checked, and
companionship in a game or on an outing.

CHOOSING FUNCTIONAL GOALS TO TEACH

Establishing functional goals begins with a thorough assessment of whether the student possesses important life skills. In the TEACCH program, we use the home, school/work, and direct observational scales from the TEACCH Transition Assessment Profile (TTAP), formerly known as the Adolescent and Adult Psychoeducational Profile (AAPEP), as our assessment tool. We also give important weight to parents' priorities for their child, the student's strengths and interests, and what a community offers as work and leisure options. Students' emerging abilities are identified and become possible goals.

Many life skills involve multiple steps so the assessment should be sufficiently specific to indicate which steps a student already knows. We often find it necessary to analyze tasks to break down the assignment into individual steps before expecting the student to be successful with the entire job. For example, to teach a student to make a fruit salad, we first teach washing, peeling, slicing, measuring, mixing, etc. as individual components before asking the student to make the salad. Once students learn the skills necessary to one task, we provide new learning opportunities so that they can practice and see the application of these same skills with new tasks, such as making a tossed salad or a smoothie drink. Then, they can apply their recently learned skills in a new setting, such as food preparation on a job in a restaurant.

DESIGNING THE TASK

What you will see pictured in *Tasks Galore for the Real World* are over 240 tasks that have visual structure components embedded in them. Visual strategies usually enable students to be independent and often make the tasks more interesting for them. Such strategies sometimes allow students to complete more sophisticated tasks even though they have not yet developed a conceptual understanding of the underlying principles and are not yet able to think abstractly or to judge appropriately.

We want students to understand what to do when they see the task. We want them to know where to begin, how to proceed, and when they are finished. We want them to look at the task and have a sense that they can be "good at it," the same sense we want to have before tackling an assignment. We break down visual strategies into three parts:
1. visual instructions,
2. visual clarity, and
3. visual organization.

VISUAL INSTRUCTIONS

Visual instructions usually tell the student the sequence in which to perform the tasks. These instructions provide the necessary information for the student to put the bits and pieces, the details, together in a coherent way. People who have an innate ability to organize can plan out the sequence themselves. People with innate logical reasoning can comprehend the meaningful pieces among all the parts and make their own decisions about how to proceed; they do not need pictures or written lists. Many people with autism spectrum disorders, however, do not think in this manner. They, therefore, need a visual "recipe" that instructs them how to proceed with the "ingredients" before them. Although visual instructions can take many forms, the guiding principle is to choose a form that is meaningful to the student. If the form is understandable, the student will be able to use it independently. The visual instructions will give the student with autism confidence to succeed with the job. Several types of visual instructions are indicated below.

   Finished product sample (This is one of the more sophisticated levels of visual instruction because the student sees how the finished product looks but must plot out the sequence to make an identical one.)
   Written instructions
   Pictures and photos with or without words
   Objects

What the different types of visual instructions have in common is that they provide the recipe for what to do with the materials and in what order.

VISUAL CLARITY

The second visual strategy we use in tasks is visual clarity. This means that we highlight some pieces of information that the students see before them. We label, for example, to indicate location or sequence, and we emphasize a part so the students will recognize that the part is relevant.

VISUAL ORGANIZATION

A third visual strategy is simply organization of the bits and pieces (the ingredients of the recipe). We want the student to look at the parts and know where each belongs because the organization of the materials makes sense. Segmented and separated materials visually organize the task. Often, a well-structured task will include more than one visual strategy, as depicted below in the photograph of flashlight assembly.

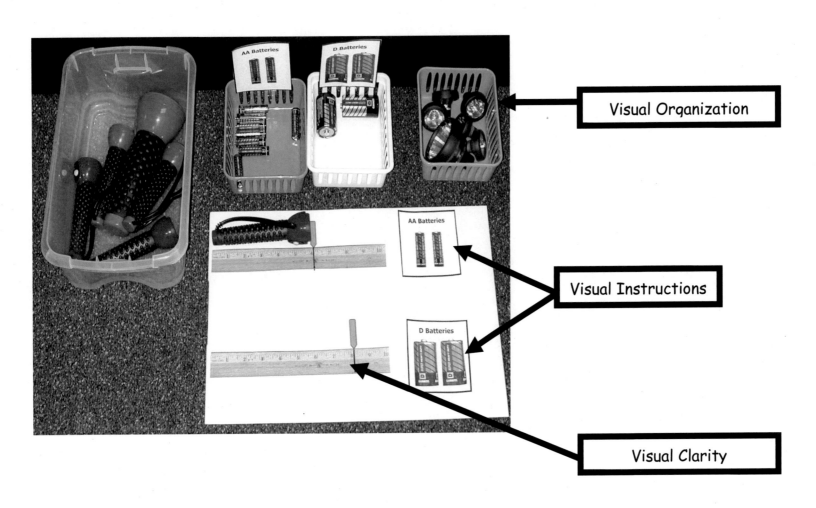

IS IT TIME TO TEACH YET?

You have done a thorough assessment of the student's strengths and interests, parent priorities, and community offerings. You have already taught the student how to use a daily schedule and a work system. You have helped the student recognize physical cues in the environment. You have done task analysis on jobs and determined the student's existing, emerging, and "too difficult for now" skills. You have established functional teaching goals for the student. You have devised a communication system and helped the student recognize situations in which communication is especially important. You have designed functional tasks so the student can look at them and see where the pieces belong, as well as screen out the insignificant parts as you visually highlight the relevant ones. You have provided visual instructions that are understandable to the student. You are truly individualizing for each student (avoiding generic strategies), so that the strategies and goals are meaningful and are being used successfully, routinely, and independently. It is time to teach the new skill.

Successful learning requires a teaching progression. The new skill is taught first in a one-to-one teaching session in the teaching "laboratory" of the classroom or home. Once mastered with close supervision from the caregiver, the student practices using the newly learned skill without direct supervision. After the student is adept and independent with the skill, it is time for that person to take this new knowledge "on the road," learning how to use the skill purposefully in the real world.

Do not let your students step outside the classroom door without their individual daily schedules and work systems. These visually structured teaching strategies, once affixed to the wall or desk, go with the students to be adapted in the new locales.

HOW IT ALL COMES TOGETHER

Our student is going to his job at the golf course. Before leaving his classroom or home, however, he knew to check his *schedule*. The schedule told him what activity was next and where to go. An object, photo, colored or black-and-white drawing, written word, calendar, or daily planner may have conveyed this schedule information. The visual cue chosen depends on what the student finds meaningful. We may have found the meaningful cue if the student puts on his golf cap (an object cue) and goes to the door or reads the written word and walks to the golf course or anticipates his ride there.

Once at the golf course, our student finds his workstation and looks for visual information, his *work system* or *to do list*.

One job on the work system or to do list is ensuring that there is a pencil and scorecard on each golf cart steering wheel. For the young man to do the task independently, a supervisor has embedded *visual structure* similar to that the student has practiced in his classroom. Our student has used checklist strategies with a vast number of different types of tasks; as a result, this student can follow visual instructions in a checklist form.

Examples of a schedule, a work system/to do list, and a visually structured task (checklist) are on the following page.

SCHEDULE	
	~~GET DRESSED~~
	GOLF COURSE
	BARBER SHOP
	LUNCH

	FILL WHEELBARROW
	CHECK DIVOT REPAIR BOTTLES
	FILL WITH SAND
	PLACE PENCILS AND SCORESHEETS IN GOLF CARTS
	WASH GOLF BALLS
	DRINK AT SNACK BAR

Golf Cart#	Score-sheet	Pencil
3	✓	✓
7		
18		
32		
26		

Schedule
Lists where to go and in what sequence

Work System/ To Do List
Shows what and how much work, progress, and what next

Visually Structured Task
Gives visual instructions and helps organize approach to task

THE TEACHING CHALLENGE

Your challenge in teaching new tasks is twofold: (1) you are teaching the skill, and. perhaps more importantly, (2) you are teaching the student to integrate the visual strategies (e.g., containers, color cues, labels, pictures, jigs, lists, etc.) into a meaningful, purposeful action. We want the student to look at the list or highlighted cue and to realize that it means he is to *do something.*

We do this by pointing out the cues and instructing the use of those cues through simple words and short phrases, which we hope the student will internalize as his own directions as he independently organizes the steps necessary to complete a task. We separate the concepts being taught within a task so that the concept and the associated language make sense to the student. Once a student sees that the cues mean taking some action, we generalize this ability to new skills using similar visual strategies. Often the materials or equipment the student will use in a new setting or in the future will not be identical to the ones he used initially. If the student has learned to *read the visual strategies*, the copier, dishwasher, or spray bottle can change, but he will still know what needs to be done and how to proceed.

AFTER CAREFUL PLANNING, WHAT IF IT DOESN'T WORK?

Even after years of experience, we rarely introduce a student to a task that does not need some type of restructuring so the student can better understand what to do. It is unlikely that any of the tasks depicted in *Tasks Galore for the Real World* will work perfectly for your students the first time. We restructure tasks so students can become independent. We usually restructure not by changing the skill we are teaching but by choosing visual strategies that are clearer, better organized, or more meaningful to the student.

We observe our students and analyze when they begin needing help. Instead of continually providing that help, however, we ask the following questions.

Does the student know how to complete the task in a systematic way?

Is the student integrating what his eyes see (the visual strategies) with some action (using the skills in the appropriate sequence)?

Does the student need additional help to focus on the relevant details?

Can the student organize the materials independently?

Then we restructure accordingly.

We asked one student to count 25 books and place them in a box. He had no difficulty reading the visual instructions or counting to 25 accurately, yet he was not completing the task in a systematic manner nor properly organizing the materials. He did not comprehend a significant facet of performing the task, neatness. A common sense, judgment issue kept him from being able to perform the task independently. Instead of our constantly monitoring and directing the student, however, we restructured the task to add visual components to compensate for this lack of judgment. We thought of a range of possible ways to restructure, from abstract to concrete:

teach the concept of neat versus messy.

more information in the written instructions, including an analogy this student might understand, such as "stack them like pancakes,"

a product sample that shows a box of neatly assembled books, and

a picture instruction in the bottom of the box.

We also remembered our rule of thumb about not asking a person with autism to concentrate on two ideas or concepts at once; we separated the job into the two different tasks: (1) counting the 25 books and then, (2) putting the books neatly into the box.

WHAT NEXT?

So, now your student is independently doing the new task in a community setting. Hooray! Yet, the work has only begun. Maintaining that skill with continued practice is important, but a caregiver is constantly asking, "What can I teach next?" or "Where and how can I teach my student to use an already mastered skill?" These questions often are addressed by adding simple changes to the tasks, such as those that follow.

Increasing stamina
Including a higher level cognitive skill
Using the same materials in a different way to encourage flexible thinking
Inserting a communication component
Adding a quality check
Practicing the skill in new settings

OUR WISHES FOR YOU

We hope you derive as much enjoyment as we do from creating tasks for your children and students. The challenge comes in figuring out what they need to know to succeed in life and how to teach those skills. The energy comes from brainstorming and collaborating on their behalf with parents, colleagues, friends, and family. The excitement comes from knowing that students with autism are capable of learning so much. The great pleasure comes from seeing them learn something new and in sharing their feelings of achievement. The joy comes from watching them quietly, when we are not teaching, so we better appreciate how they think and what they find important and fun. From these moments of contemplative observation, we learn much about how to teach the students successfully. We hope that some of our tasks and experiences help you, but we especially wish for you these moments of energy, excitement, pleasure, joy, and quiet contemplation.

Domestic Skills

Adapted Recipes
Cleaning
Cooking
Kitchen Utensils
Laundry
Pet Care
Putting Things Away
Recycling
Setting Table
Sweeping
Washing Dishes

Domestic Skills – Adapted Recipes

Make Oatmeal with a
Flip Book Photo Recipe

MAKING OATMEAL

Make Oatmeal Following
a Photo Card Recipe
(Turn Over Card When Finished)

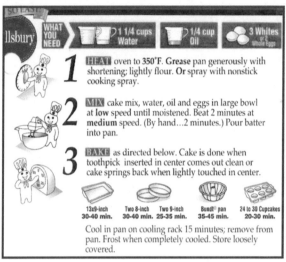

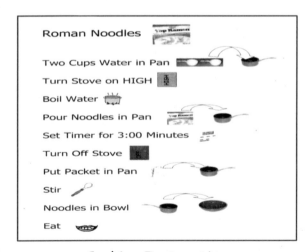

Roman Noodles

Two Cups Water in Pan

Turn Stove on HIGH

Boil Water

Pour Noodles in Pan

Set Timer for 3:00 Minutes

Turn Off Stove

Put Packet in Pan

Stir

Noodles in Bowl

Eat

Cooking Instructions
(Top to Bottom Checklist)

Color Code Knobs
(Green Paper Highlights Correct Burner)

I. Get and put on counter:

> _____ 1 measuring cup
> _____ 2 eggs
> _____ 8 inch round cake pans
> _____ oil
> _____ large mixing bowl
> _____ small bowl
> _____ mixer
> _____ 2 beaters for mixer
> _____ rubber spatula
> _____ cooking spray
> _____ timer
> _____ oven mitts
> _____ 2 plates
> _____ wire racks

Adapted Cake Recipe

Domestic Skills – Cleaning

Dust Top to Bottom,
Using Colored Dots

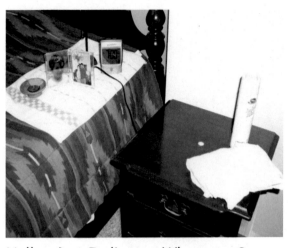

Yellow Dot Indicates Where to Spray,
and Towel Indicates
Where to Place Items from Table

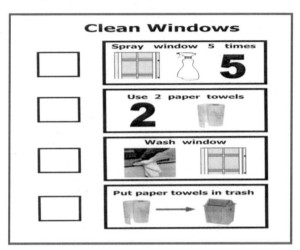

Clean Windows Following a
Pictured Written Checklist

Baking Soda Highlights Need to
Vacuum and Direction of Cleaning

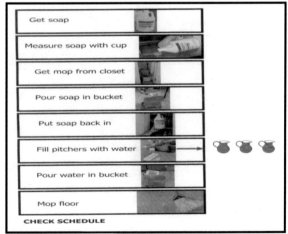

Mopping Pictured Written Checklist
(The Three Pitchers Indicate Quantity)

Dots on Windows Indicate Where
and How Much to Spray

Domestic Skills – Cleaning Tables

Wash a Small Placemat
(Limiting the Space)

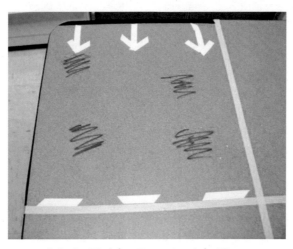

Limit Table Space with Tape,
Making the Dirty Areas More Obvious
(Arrows Indicate Directions)

Dots on Table for Spraying Cleaner
(One-to-One Correspondence
Dots Made with Washable Markers)

Sponge Bob© Work System
for Washing Tables and Chairs

Match Cards from
Sponge Bob© Work System

Number Work System for
Washing Multiple Tables

Domestic Skills - Cooking

Scanned Picture of Thumb and Fingers
for Proper Placement on Can Opener

Red Chip Counting System for
Cups of Water to Make Lemonade

Make Lemonade, Left to Right
(Visual Cue for Water Level)

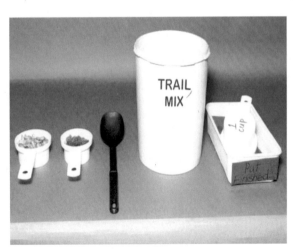

Pour and Stir Trail Mix,
Left to Right

Picture Card Recipe
to Make Smoothie

Domestic Skills - Cooking

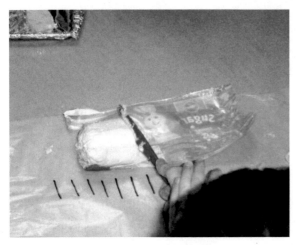

Cut Cookie Dough
(Lined Cutting Jig)

Place Cookie on Cookie Sheet
(1:1 with Nonstick Spray)

Place Cookies on Cookie Sheet
(1:1 Correspondence with Chocolate Chip)

Make a Bologna Sandwich with
Flip Book Instructions

Velcro™ Cards to Make Popcorn
(Match Card with Microwave Button)

Peanut Butter and Jelly Sandwich
(Left-to-Right Cut-Out Photos)

Domestic Skills – Kitchen Utensils

Put Away Spoons Left to Right
(Cover Extra Compartments)

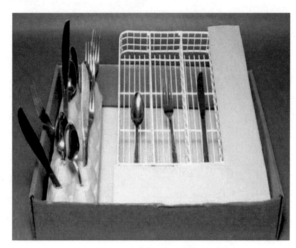

Sort Silverware
(Stabilize and Segment in Egg Carton)

Hang Utensils,
Matching with Jigs

Sort Knives and Forks,
Matching with Concrete Samples

Roll Silverware,
Using a Silhouette Jig

Domestic Skills - Laundry

Sort Laundry, Following
Pictured Written Labels

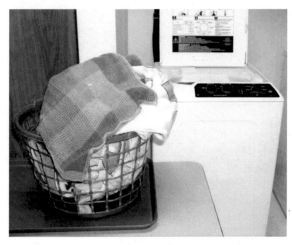

Load Washer,
Left to Right

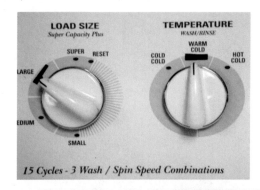

Fold Laundry, Using a
Flip and Fold Device

Put Laundry in Drawers,
Matching Black-and-White Photos

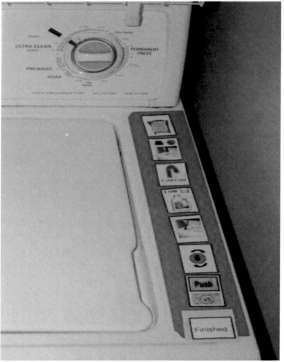

Wash Laundry
(Top to Bottom Pictured Cards and
Color-Coded Knobs)

Domestic Skills – Pet Care

Spray Water on Chameleon
Clothespin Counting System

Feed Dog
(Two Green Cups Full)

Feed Fish
Food Pre-portioned for Each Day

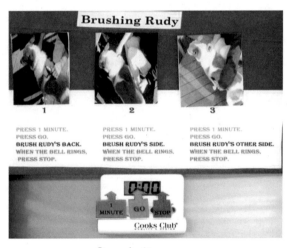

Brush Dog
Pictured Written Instructions

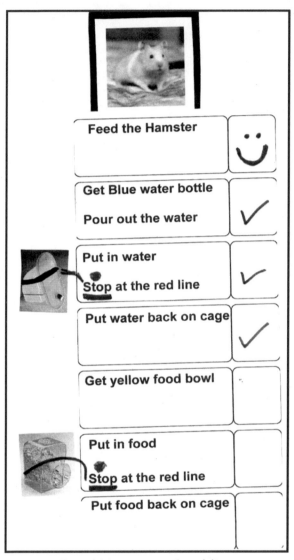

Feed Hamster Checklist
(Color Cues for Quantity)

Domestic Skills – Putting Away Kitchen Things

Hang Cups
(One-to-One Correspondence)

Put Away Dishes,
Matching Pictured Written Cues

Put Away Sodas,
Matching Colored Boxes and Cans

Put Away Dishes,
Sorting Short and Tall Glasses

Sort Pictures by Location,
Pantry or Refrigerator

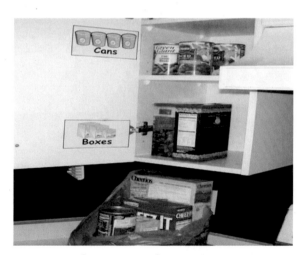

Put Away Groceries,
Sorting Boxes and Cans

Domestic Skills - Recycling

Sort Trash and Dishes,
Following Pictured Written Cues

Sort Trash and Recycling,
Following Object Written Cue

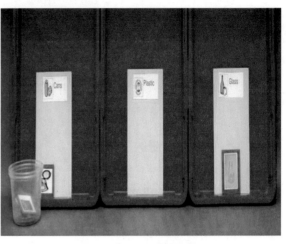

Sort Recycling by
Cans, Plastic, and Glass Pictures

Sort Cans and Paper
with a Cut-Out Jig

Sort Glass, Tin, and Plastic,
Following Photos, Objects, and
Words

Place Recycling Bin Outside,
Using Fencing as Physical Boundary

Domestic Skills – Setting the Table

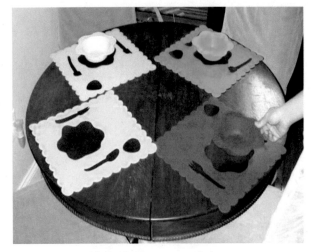

Match Items with
Silhouette Placemats

Match Picture Work System to Set the Table

Items for Setting the Table
Organized in a Basket

Product Sample Picture Instruction

Flip Book for Collecting Dishes to Set Table
(Mark Box for Each Item Collected)

Domestic Skills - Sweeping

Sweep Lanes into Red Rectangle,
then Sweeping into Dustpan

Sweep Counter into Dustpan

Make Dirt More Obvious,
Sweeping into Red, "X" Box

Color Code Broom Handle
(Match Color to Colored Wristbands)

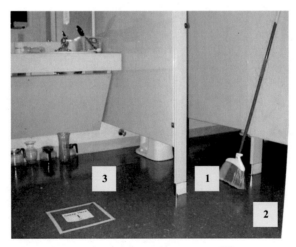

Numbered Sticky Notes on Floor
Sequence Sweeping
(Sweep to Yellow Box)

Sweep Numbered Stalls
Checklist

Domestic Skills – Washing Dishes

Wash Dishes from Left to Right
(Dishes Separated into Containers),
then Watch Nemo© Movie

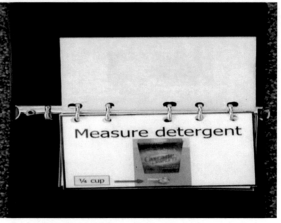

Dishwasher Flip Book

Dishwasher Checklist

Limit Dishwashing to
One Type of Item

Wash Dishes Work System
(with Pictured Written Cards)

Independent Functioning

Budgeting
Calendar
Clothes
Grocery Shopping
Hygiene
Lunch Choices
Money
Nutrition/Exercise
Packing
Telephone
Telling Time
Temperature
Time Management
Vocabulary Concepts

Independent Functioning – Budgeting

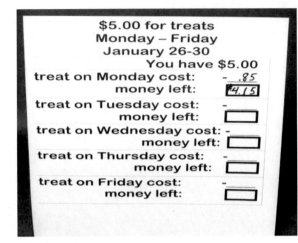

Budget Weekly Allowance

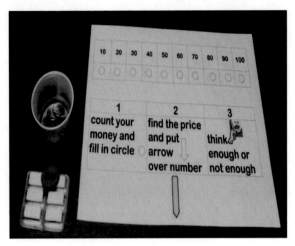

Budget Worksheet

Use "Dollar Line" to Determine if
There is Enough Money
to Purchase Items

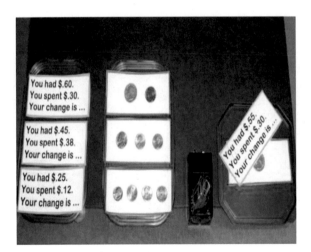

Matching Written Amount
to Amount with Coins

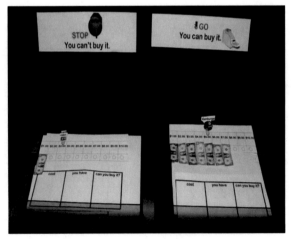

Use Worksheet to Determine
if There is Enough Money to Buy

Match Price with Dollars,
Using One-Up Method
(Dollars Plus One Dollar for Cents)

Independent Functioning - Calendar

Sequence Today and Tomorrow

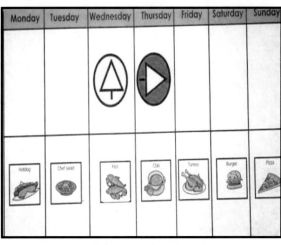

Weekly Meal Calendar
(Symbols for Today and Tomorrow)

Write Date on Foods

File Holidays by Corresponding Month

Book About Weekend Visit

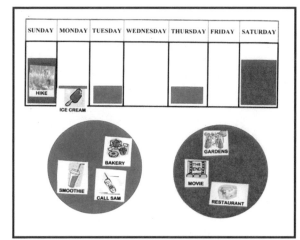

Leisure Calendar
Color Coded for Weekend and
Weekday Activities

Independent Functioning - Clothes

Match Clothes with the Scene

Dress the Person According
to the Season

Sort Summer and Winter Clothes

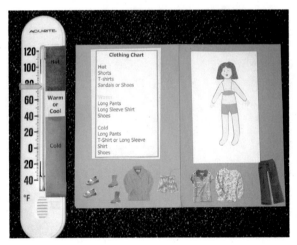

Dress the Person According to the
Temperature and Chart

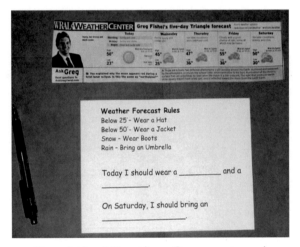

Read the Weather Forecast and
Make Decisions About Clothing

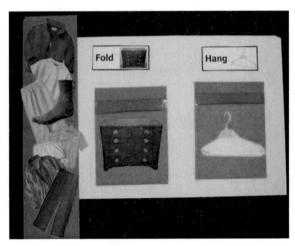

Sort Clothes
(Fold or Hang)

Independent Functioning - Grocery Shopping

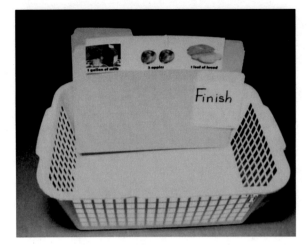

Grocery List on Cards
and Finished Pocket

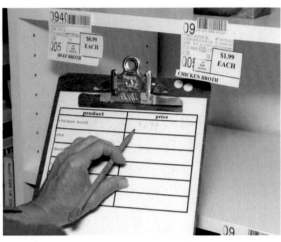

Locate Prices

Grocery Category Lotto

Match Groceries to Category

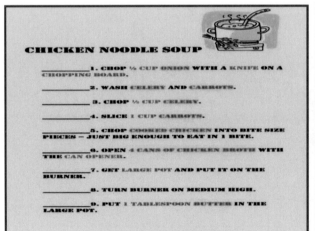

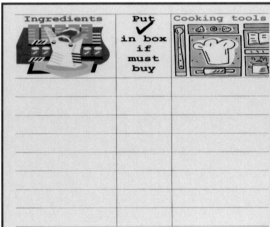

Create an Ingredient and Shopping List from a Recipe

Independent Functioning – Grocery Shopping

Pictured Written Cards Shopping List

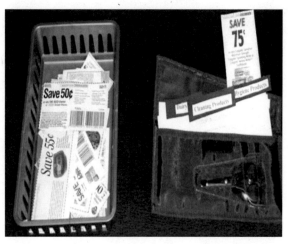

File Coupons by Grocery Categories

Photograph Shopping List and Finished Pocket

Develop a Shopping List

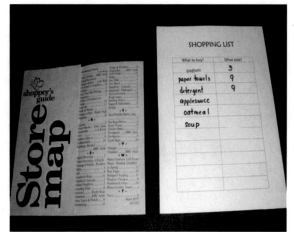

Shopping List with Store Map
(Locate Corresponding Aisle)

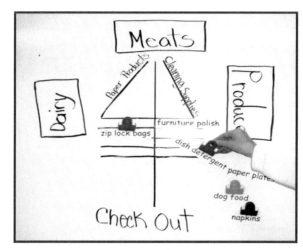

Store Layout
(Place Magnet in Correct Section)

Independent Functioning - Hygiene

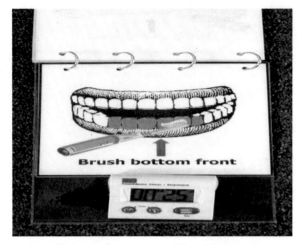

Tooth Brushing Flip Book
(Each Section of Teeth Highlighted on
Separate Pages)

Shaving Sequence,
Using Colored Numbers

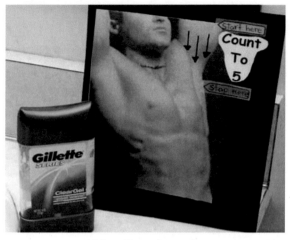

Use Deodorant
(Pictured Written Cue)

Body Part Picture Cards for Bathing
and Finished Box

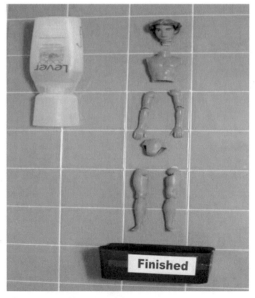

Top-to-Bottom Object Cue
for Bathing

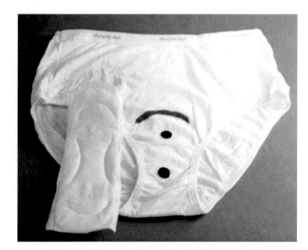

Visual Cues for Pad Placement

Independent Functioning – Lunch Choices

Match Food Items
with Scanned Photos

Lunch Choices with Photos
Velcro™ Choice in Box

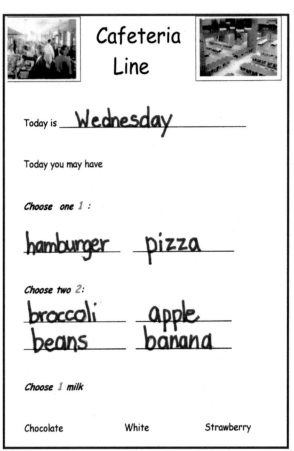

Make Lunch Choices
on Written List

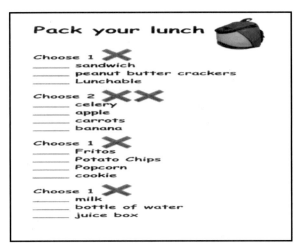

Mark Lunch Choices
on Written List

Velcro™ Lunch Choice
Flip Book

Independent Functioning - Money

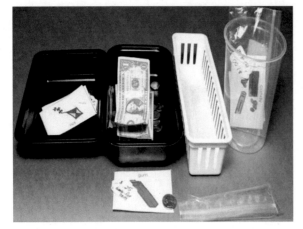

Match Dollars and Coins with
Written Value

Make Change,
Using Designated Coins

Match Dollars and Coins with
Written Amount of Money

Find Prices on the Menu,
Totaling Cost of Order

Match Prices by Rounding
to Closest Dollar Amount

Using Money in Meaningful Context
(School Candy Fundraiser)

Independent Functioning – Money

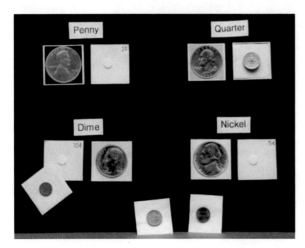

Match Coins with Scanned Picture

Match Coins with Jig
(Separate Envelopes in Wallet)

Cafeteria Purchase
(Matching Money with a Picture Jig)

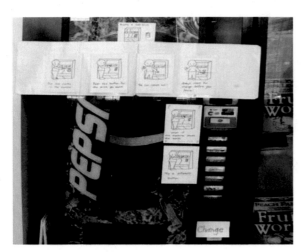

Pictured Written Steps for Using
the Vending Machine

Calculate Amounts of Money,
Following Written Instructions

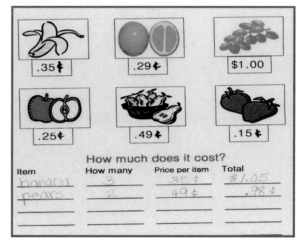

Money Calculation Worksheet
(Purchasing Multiple Quantities)

Independent Functioning – Nutrition and Exercise

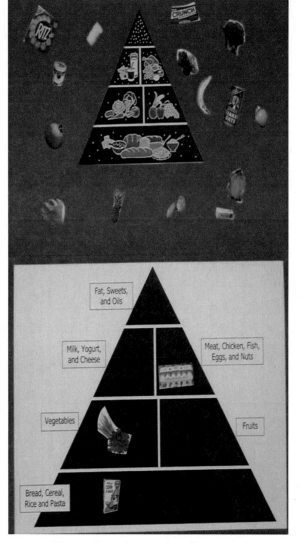

Place Foods on the Pyramid

Sort Vegetables and Entrees

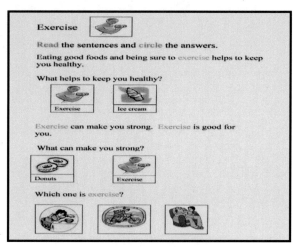

Exercise and Health

Running Lap Work System,
Using Chips to Count Number of Laps

Sort Healthy and Junk Foods

Independent Functioning - Packing

Pack Swim Bag,
Matching Items with Photo

Pack Lunch Box,
Matching Items with Photos

Checklist for Packing Swim Bag

Written Instructions,
Packing Backpack for School

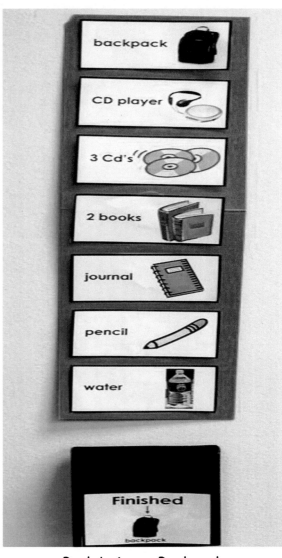

Pack Leisure Backpack
(Written Pictured Cards with
Finished Box)

Independent Functioning - Telephone

Script for Answering the Telephone

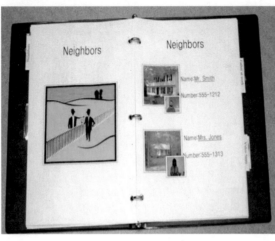

Personal Telephone Directory

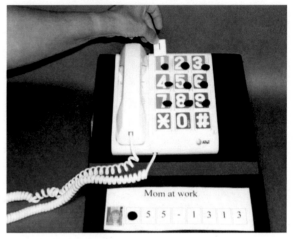

Match Veclro™ Numbers to Dial a Phone Number

Concept of When to Communicate Problems

Whom to Call in Various Situations Flip Book

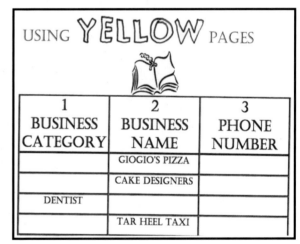

Yellow Pages Worksheet

Independent Functioning – Telling Time

Match Digital and Analog Time

Add Time

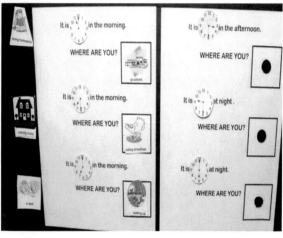

Match Time of Day with Activity

Sort Daytime and Nighttime Activities

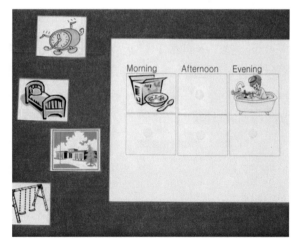

Sort Activities by Times of Day

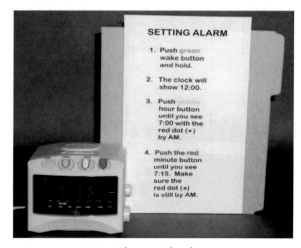

Set Alarm Clock, Following Written Instructions

Independent Functioning –Temperature

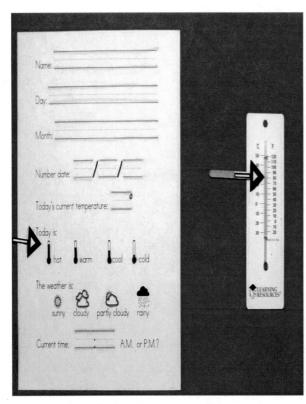

Read the Temperature and
Complete a Worksheet

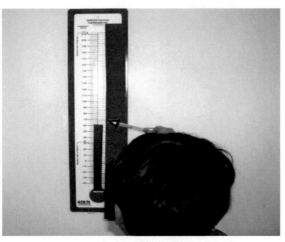

Read the Classroom Thermometer,
Using an Arrow Pointer

Set the Bathtub Temperature,
Matching Colored Tape Markings

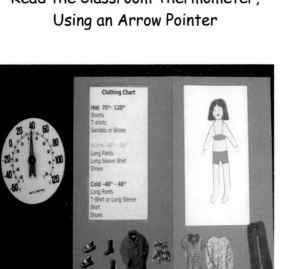

Select Clothing Based on
the Temperature

Check Temperature in Storeroom,
Using Written and Pictured Instructions

Independent Functioning – Time Management

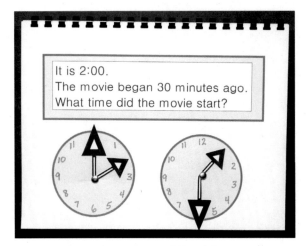

Complete Word Problems,
Using Time

Adapt Speed to the
Available Amount of Time

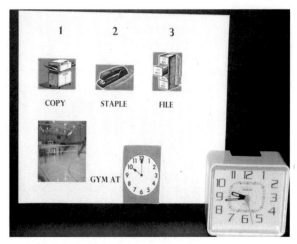

End an Activity Based on Time

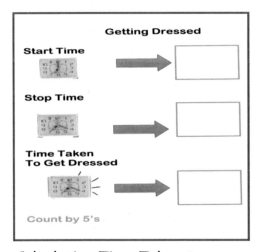

Calculating Time Taken to
Complete a Task

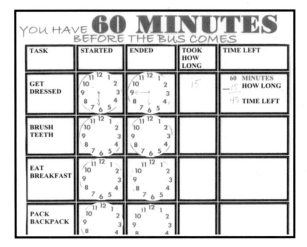

Budgeting Time Worksheet

Manage Time for Break Activity

Independent Functioning – Vocabulary Concepts

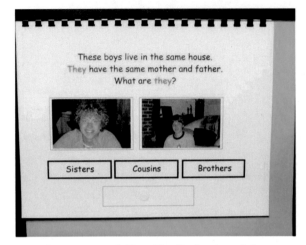

Concept of Family Relationships

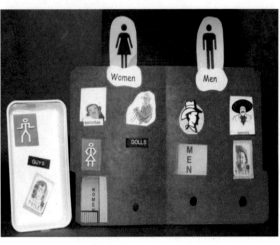

Men's and Women's Restrooms

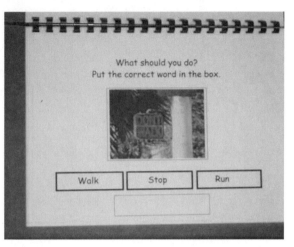

Meaning of Community Signs and Symbols

Sort by Amount in Bottle

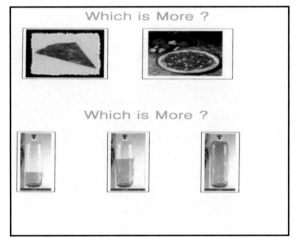

Concept of More Worksheet

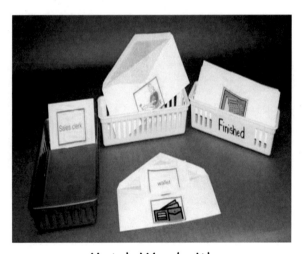

Match Word with Community Vocabulary Picture

Vocational Skills

Assembly
Filing
Collecting Materials
Measuring Length
Measuring Weight and Volume
Office Equipment
Quality Control
Sorting
Stocking/Inventory
Using Tools

Vocational Skills - Assembly

Assemble Flags
(Photo Instructions)

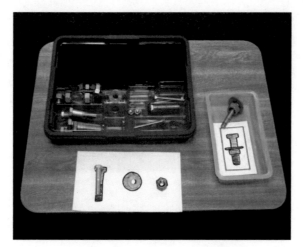

Assemble Nuts and Bolts
(Left-to-Right Jig Scanned to Size)

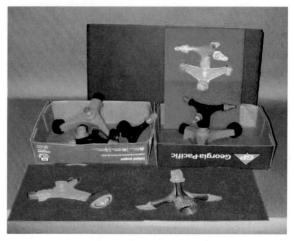

Assemble Sprinkler

Place Flowers in Vase, Left-to-Right
(One-to-One Correspondence)

Water Flowers
(Empty Containers Go in Red Can)

Place Vase on Table,
Matching Picture on Table

Vocational Skills – Collecting Materials

Collect Mail in Bag
with Scanned Photo of Mailbox

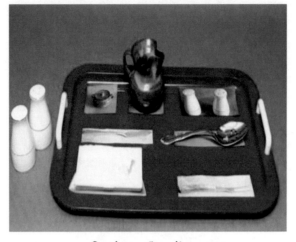

Gather Condiments,
Matching Scanned Photos

GET BASKET AND PUT IN

_____ 1 glass cleaner

_____ 1 seat cleaner

_____ 2 table cleaners

_____ 3 clean towels

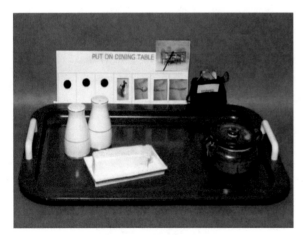

Gather Condiments
(Pictured Card System,
Finished Pocket to Right)

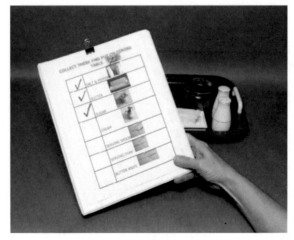

Gather Condiments
(Pictured Written Checklist)

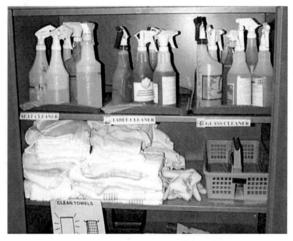

Collect Cleaning Supplies
(Written Checklist and
Labeled Supply Closet)

Vocational Skills – Filing

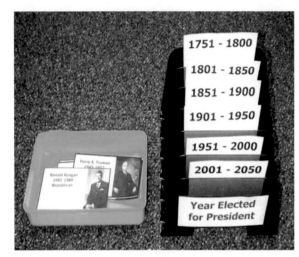

File Presidents within Time Frame
of Their Presidency

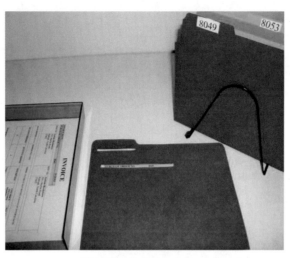

File Purchase Orders by
Five-Digit Number
(Template Blocks Distractions)

File Folders by
Color and Label

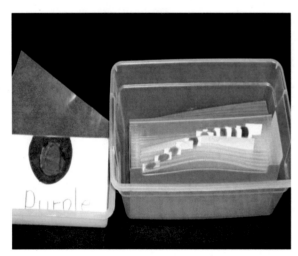

File by Color Cue

File by Second Letter,
Using Color Cue

Sort Mail by
Bills, Medical, and Junk

Vocational Skills – Measuring Length

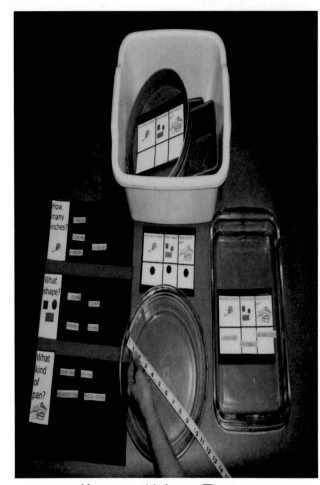

Measure Using a Tape,
Identify Length, Shape, and Type of Pans

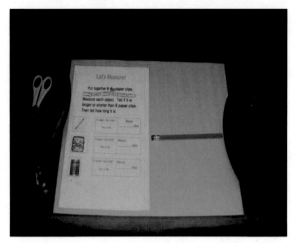

Measure Objects and Record Their
Length on the Worksheet

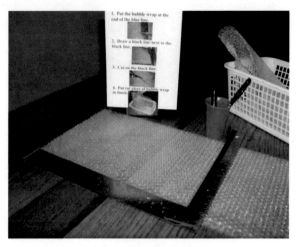

Cut Bubble Wrap,
Following Pictured Written Instructions

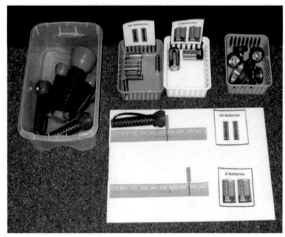

Measure Flashlights and Insert
Corresponding Batteries
(Arrows Clarify Length)

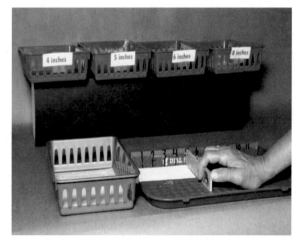

Measure Pieces of Paper and
Sort by Length

Vocational Skills – Measuring Weight or Volume

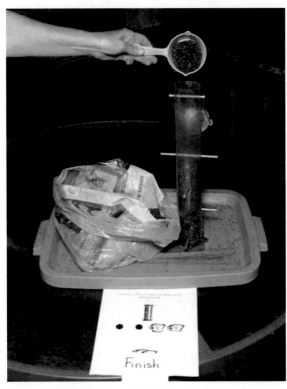

Fill Bird Feeder, Using Cut-Out Measuring Cups as a Counting System

Measure by Weight, Using Arrows to Highlight Correct Weight

Fill Bird Feeder with Scoop, Moving Left to Right

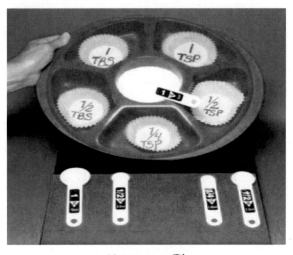

Measure Flour, Matching Amounts with Corresponding Measuring Spoons

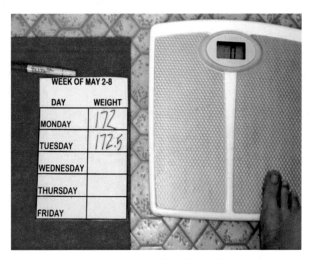

Record Body Weight, Using a Digital Scale

Vocational Skills - Office Equipment

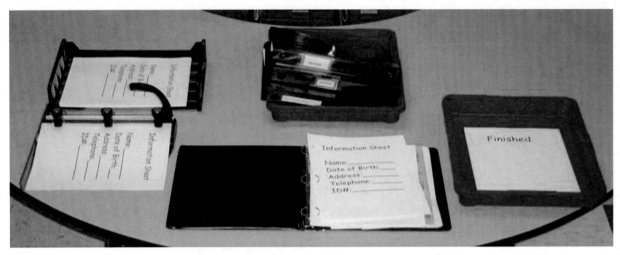

Hole-Punch Packets for Notebooks
(Align Packet with Red Ruler Before Punching Holes)

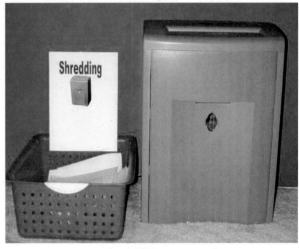

Shred Paper,
Left to Right

Color Code Buttons on Copier
(Colors Correspond to Instructions)

Segment Pages,
Highlighting Where to Staple

Make Copies,
Following Quantity Checklist

Vocational Skills - Quality Control Sorting

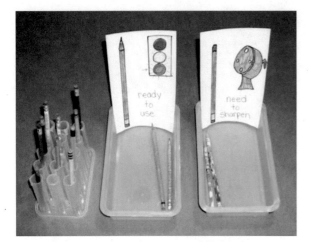

Sort Pencils Using Visual Cues,
Ready to Use or Need Sharpening

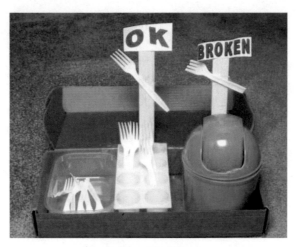

Sort Plastic Forks,
Intact (OK) or Broken

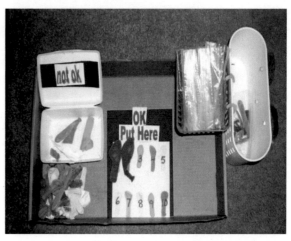

Package Balloons by Picture Jig and
Sort Those "not OK"

Sort Dirty and Clean Dishes

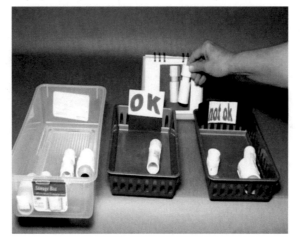

Sort Plumbing Assembly,
Comparing to Scanned Sample

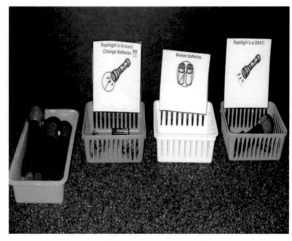

Sort Flashlights,
Replacing Batteries in "Broken"
Flashlights

Vocational Skills - Sorting

Hang Clothes by Category
(Picture Dictionary)

Match Word with Picture
(Kitchen Vocabulary)

Sort Coupons (Barcode) and
Advertisements (No Barcode)

Sort Magazines

Vocational Skills – Stocking/Inventory

Pictured Written Inventory Checklist

Match Item with Photo
(Dots Indicate Amount to Stock)
and Line Up Items with Black Line

Stock Pastries by Scanned Photo

Stock CDs
(Start and Finish Visual Cues)

Stock Milk,
Matching Cap Color with Sign Color

Front Cans

Vocational Skills - Tools

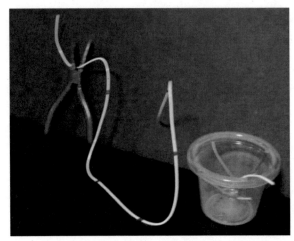

Needle-Nose Pliers to Cut Wire

Hammer to Pound in Plastic Pegs

Screwdriver to Assemble
Electric Sockets

Organize Wrenches by Size

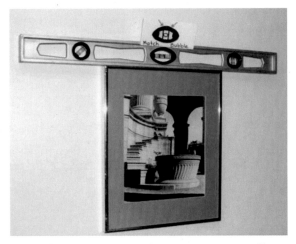

Level to Adjust Pictures on Wall

Clippers to Cut Dead Flowers,
Matching Sample on Bag

Job Sites

Potential Job Sites:

Church
Garden Center
*Golf Course
*Grocery Store
Hospital
Hotel
Laundry
*Library
Mail Room
*Non-Profit Organization
Pet Store/Animal Shelter
*Restaurant/Cafeteria
*Retail Store
*School (see transition)
School Warehouse

Sites Demonstrated in this Book

Transition

Maintenance	Clerical	Food Service	General
Clean Mirrors/Windows	Check Out Library Books Stamp Due Dates	Clean Tables	Bake and Sell Goods
Clean Sinks	Collate/Copy/Organize Teachers' Materials	Prepare Food	Collect and Put Away Empty Drink Bottles/Cans
Dust	Collate Newsletters	Serve Food	Do Contract Work
Empty Trash	Collect Attendance Sheets	Put Away Chairs	Deliver Supplies
Prepare Fields	File	Put Up Menu or Write It on Board	Do Laundry/Fold Towels Assist in Art/P.E. Classes
Mop Halls (Using Industrial Materials)	Perform Printing/Copying Jobs	Stock Napkins, Utensils, Trays, etc.	Fill Drink Machines
Straighten Areas Pick Up Trash	Sort Teachers' Mail	Sort Silverware	Inventory Supplies
Sweep Halls (Using Industrial Equipment)	Shelve Returned Books Collect Books Left on Tables	Stack and Dump Trays	Handle Non-Profit Organization Mailings
Vacuum Classrooms/ Offices	Shred Confidential Materials	Sweep Cafeteria	Recycle
Weed flower beds	Straighten Newspapers	Take Out Trash from Cafeteria	Clerk in School Store
Water Plants	Type for Teachers/Office	Wash Dishes (by Hand/ in Dishwasher)	Sort/Put Away Art Room Supplies

When students become adolescents, it is important to begin considering their "transition" (i.e., their goals beyond secondary education). These examples of in-school jobs may be very beneficial in preparing students for future jobs in the community.

Job Sites - Gardening

Water Plants, Matching Colored
Bottles to Color on Pot
(Water Pre-poured)

Water Plants inside
Hula Hoops

Mow Lawn within Four Cones

Water Plants,
Matching Number and Color to
Watering Cup

Pull Weeds Inside
Hula Hoops

Water Plants
with Funnel

Job Sites - Library

Clear Tables and
Put Books in Finished Basket

Sort Picture Books by
Easy or Fiction

Sort Videos by Topics
(Plant, Bird, and Mammal Cues)

Place Books on Shelves,
Arranged on the Black Visual Cue

Practice Marking Through
the Bar Code

Mark Through the Barcode and
Place in Finished Box

Job Sites – Restaurant/Cafeteria

Fill Cups with Ice
and Put Them into Blue Cooler

Organize Clean Trays
(One-to-One Correspondence)

Wash Tables,
then Replace Condiments

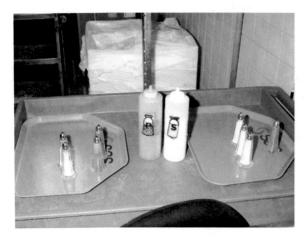

Fill Salt and Pepper Shakers

Stock Food,
Matching Photographs

Roll Silverware,
(Left to Right)

Job Site – School Office

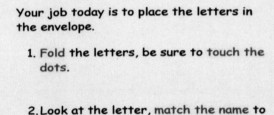

Your job today is to place the letters in the envelope.

1. Fold the letters, be sure to touch the dots.

2. Look at the letter, match the name to the envelope.

3. Put the envelope into the finished box.

Fold Paper and Stuff Envelopes,
Using Written and Color

Collect Mail from Teacher's Box,
Matching the Label

Product Sample for Collating Packets
(Side-by-Side Work Stations)

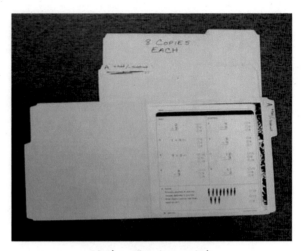

Make Copies with
Original Attached to Folder

Place Address Labels and Stamps,
Using a Template